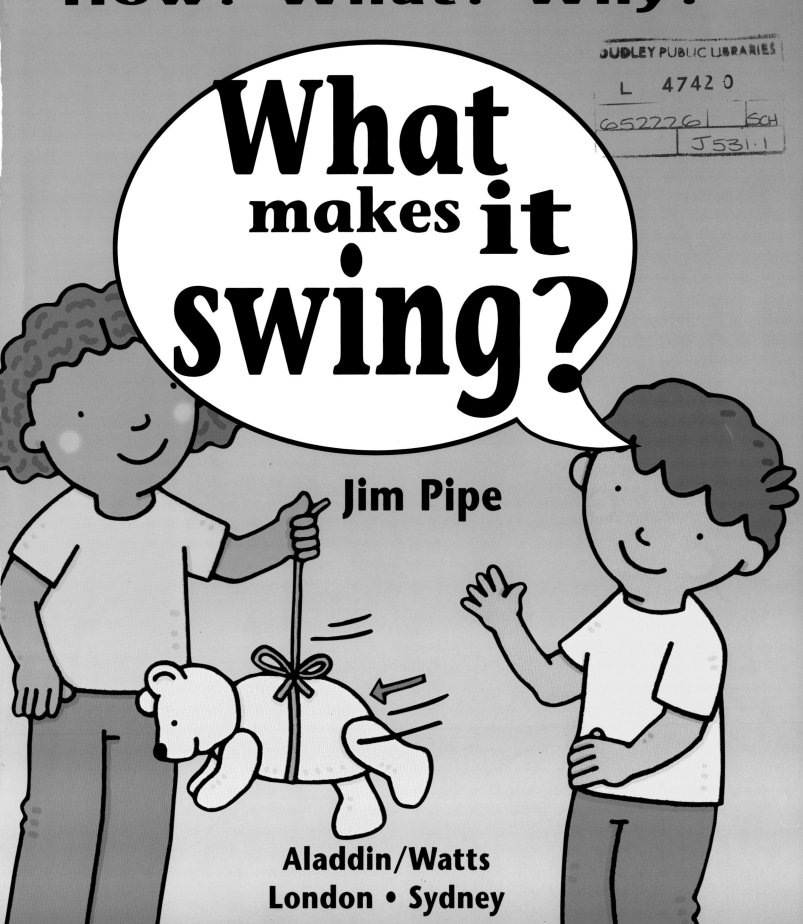

What makes it swing?

Jim Pipe

Aladdin/Watts

London • Sydney

How can you make it move?

Steve, Amy, Jo and Zack are playing in the park with Zack's truck. Zack gets in first and the others help him to get moving.

Let's see how the children find out.

A kick from behind works, too. Look at the truck go!

Not too hard! You might dent it.

3

So pushes and pulls start things moving. A kick does, too. It's like a hard push.

Why it works

Everything needs a push or a pull to make it start moving. Pushes and pulls are called forces. A push is a force which makes things move away from you.

A kick is a sort of push. A pull is also a force, but it moves things towards you. What pushes and pulls are there when you swim, play tennis or ride a bike?

Solve the puzzle!

Why shouldn't Steve kick the truck? Take a paper cup and see what pushes, pulls and kicks can do to its shape.

5

What makes a swing change direction?

At the playground, Jo gets on the tyre. Steve gives her a push to make her swing. Zack also wants to give her a push, but the tyre is going in the wrong direction.

Can we make Jo swing over to Zack?

I think a push from the side will make Jo change direction.

6

7

Let's see how the children find out.

8

3

Pushes can also make it swing in a circle.

But a push on only one side makes it spin round and round.

Why it works

When something is moving in a straight line, a push or pull from the side makes it change direction. Pushes and pulls can also make things spin or move in a circle. Think about a ball. You can kick it in a straight line, and then you can make it change direction with another kick. You can also make it spin by twisting it with your hand.

4

Solve the puzzle

How can a puppy make you walk in circles? Think about what happens if you have a puppy on a lead and it wants to go in a different direction to you.

9

How do you make a roundabout speed up?

The children are playing on the roundabout. Steve and Amy get on and Zack gives them a push.

Let's see how the children find out.

Why it works

A push or a pull makes things start to move. An extra push or pull in the same direction makes them go faster. Pushing things harder also makes them speed up. So pushing a roundabout harder makes it spin faster. But a push or pull in the opposite direction makes things slow down and go the other way.

Solve the puzzle

Are things easier to push when they get heavier? Try adding wooden bricks to a toy truck one at a time. Does it get easier or harder to push ?

If I push it the other way, it slows down then turns the other way. Look!

So a bigger push must make a roundabout spin faster, too. But a push in the opposite direction makes it slow down and stop.

3

13

Why don't you slide up a slide?

The children queue up to go on the slide. Amy goes first. She climbs up the steps then sits down at the top. When she lets go, Amy whizzes down to the bottom of the slide.

Why do you always slide down?

15

Let's see how the children find out.

When I let go from the top of the ramp, the car goes faster.

3

It's going further, too. The longer slope must mean the force is pulling the car for longer.

Why it works

When you sit on a slide, you slide down. If you throw a ball into the air, it falls to the ground. These things happen because of a force which pulls everything down to the ground. We call this force gravity. You can't see it, but gravity is pulling on you all the time. Without it, we would float around like astronauts in space.

Solve the puzzle

Do heavy things fall faster? Make two balls of plasticine, one twice as big as the other. Drop them from the same height at the same time. Which hits the ground first? **17**

Why does a kite fly?

The wind starts to blow, so the children play with Steve's kite. Zack lets go of the kite and it flies up into the air. Steve holds onto the string so it doesn't fly away.

Why does a kite fly? I can't see anything pushing it.

It must be the wind pushing against the kite. I have to hold on tight.

Let's see how the children find out.

I can also make my whirligig spin by blowing on it.

3

So moving air can push things and make them move, even though you can't see it.

Why it works

Wind is moving air. Though you can't see it, it can push against things. On a windy day, you can feel the wind pushing against you when you walk along, and you can often see it blowing leaves along the ground. The same force pushes a kite up into the sky and makes a whirligig spin round and round.

Solve the puzzle!

Can moving water push things? Think about waves on a beach or being squirted with a hose.

21

Did you solve the puzzles?

Why shouldn't Steve kick the truck?

Pushes and pulls make things move, but they can also make things change shape or break. A hard push like a kick can squash a paper cup or dent a truck. Take a lump of plasticine and see how pulls and pushes can bend, twist and stretch it.

How can a puppy make you walk in circles?

A young dog on a lead doesn't always want to go the same way as the person taking it for a walk. It can pull you from side to side, making it hard to walk in a straight line! A strong wind can also blow you in different directions and make it hard to walk straight.

Are heavier things easier to push?

No. The heavier something gets, the harder it is to push. If you add bricks to a truck, it needs a harder push to make it move. A heavy object like a roundabout is also harder to stop when it is moving.

Do things fall faster if they are heavier?

No. If you let go of the big and small balls of plasticine at the same time, they hit the ground together. What happens when you drop them from higher up? (Think about the car on page 17).

Can moving water push things?

Yes. Moving water can push with a strong force. If someone squirts you with a hose, you can feel the force of the water. A big wave on a beach can easily knock you over. Before there were engines, people used the force of water to drive machines. Water from a river pushed on the paddles of a big waterwheel and made it spin around.

Index

© Aladdin Books Ltd 2002

Designed and produced by
Aladdin Books Ltd
28 Percy Street
London W1T 2BZ

First published in
Great Britain in 2002 by
Franklin Watts
96 Leonard Street
London EC2A 4XD

ISBN 0 7496 4742 6

A catalogue record for this book is
available from the British Library.

Printed in U.A.E.
All rights reserved

Literacy Consultant
Jackie Holderness
Westminster Institute of Education
Oxford Brookes University

Science Consultants
Helen Wilson and David Coates
Westminster Institute of Education
Oxford Brookes University

Science Tester
Alex Laar

Design
Flick, Book Design and Graphics

Illustration
Jo Moore

For Chloé Guerif